EUROPA ⚔ MILITARIA N° 11

THE FRENCH FOREIGN LEGION IN ACTION

TEXT AND PHOTOS BY
Yves DEBAY

TRANSLATED BY
JEAN-PIERRE VILLAUME

Windrow & Greene

LEGIONNAIRES
PARAS

2e REP

The war-song of the 2e Régiment Etranger de Parachutistes begins with the words ' We are the men for the shock attack ' — and their combat record supports this boast. Specialists in parachute insertion, the 'REP men' certainly rank among the world's best soldiers.

All over Europe, thousands of teenagers have dreamt of becoming paras with the famed REP, but they will need a lot of willpower for their dream to come true. The brilliant intervention at Kolwezi in 1978 and the public image of the airborne Légionnaire are responsible for this infatuation.

Their fatigues are tailored to an impeccable fit, their muscles hard and prominent, their gait supple, and their attitude marked by the cockiness that permeates their everyday activities. To the public at large, the REP men combine the feline qualities and the expertise of the para with the traditions, devotion to duty and mystery surrounding the Légion.

Certainly, the Legion unit that appeals the most to Frenchmen and foreigners alike is 2e REP and most volunteers want to serve in its ranks — especially British volunteers. Not content with enjoying a well-deserved reputation for professionalism, the REP also has the distinction of being on round-the-clock readiness. The regiment did not take part in the 1991 Gulf war but has recently performed several missions in Africa, namely in Rwanda, Tchad and Djibouti; mere routine for a formation that has one or two companies permanently posted on the 'Dark Continent'.

Apart from its world-wide 'fire brigade rôle', 2e REP is training constantly to keep fit for its '*raison d'être*': airborne intervention within the framework of FAR. 'To be ready to intervene anywhere, anytime and to win', sums up the spirit of the Légionnaires and their officers. To achieve this goal, training is permanent and intensive. The weak-willed or faint-hearted leave the regiment.

When shown around the Raffali barracks, the visitor or the military attaché often shows surprise and enquires: '*Where are they* ?' And the answer comes: 1st Coy is in Tchad, 2nd Coy in the Alps, 3rd Coy in Djibouti, CEA (Recce and Sup-

(*continued on page 9*)

REP paras specialise in parachute insertion and the drops must be short and brutal. The regiment has its own dropping zone and practice jumps are made frequently.
Every other week, an *Armée de l'Air* Transall C-160 is sent to Calvi, Corsica, for training jumps.

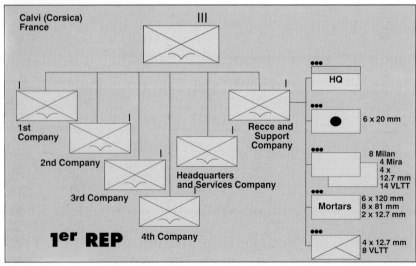

Above, left:
Scaling a bluff in Corsica, a sniper inches his way up for a better grip. Mountaineering is a good school for self confidence and courage. 2nd Company specialises in mountain training and several of its instructors come from Switzerland or Austria.

Above:
**2nd REP badges. From top to bottom:
— 1st Company
— 3rd Company
— 2nd Company
— 4th Company.**

Opposite:
Kits must be thoroughly checked before each operation. During training Exercise Fregate 88, 2e REP members inspect their packs prior to boarding an *Armée de l'Air* Transall. The operation was carried out from Toulouse-Francazal air base, in Southern France.

Right:
3rd Company paras, the regiment's amphibious specialists, speeding towards a beach during a training exercise carried out jointly with American forces. They are riding 'rigid raiders' provided by the US Marine Corps.

Far right:
A 4th Company demolition specialist team at work in desert conditions.

Below:
Sheltering behind a stone wall, a bazooka team about to fire. This 89mm anti-tank rocket launcher is higly appreciated for light anti-tank combat.

Bottom right:
At the rim of a crevasse, a 2nd Company Légionnaire provides covering fire for his comrades advancing on skis. 2nd Coy has specialised in mountain fighting and every year spends a few winter months in the Alps.

LRAC 89 mm
(Anti-tank rocket launcher)

Like all airborne infantry regiments, 2e REP is trained for light anti-tank fighting, especially in wooded or urban areas. For close anti-tank fighting in the 100/600m bracket, REP has one LRAC per combat section (5 per platoon).

Simple to use, the rocket launcher fires a projectile capable of piercing 40mm of armour plating from a 300m range. Weighing 8kg (loaded), it is operated by two men. In Central Europe, the REP also uses 120mm Apilas ' use and discard' heavy launchers capable of taking on any armoured vehicle at short range.

Both types of weapon have been designed for tackling armour at close range, and require crews with nerves of steel. There is no shortage of these in the REP. ❑

port Coy) is on firing practice in France and 4th Coy is out there mountaineering, some two days' walk from here'.

The REP belongs to the 11th Parachute Division and is based at Camp Raffali in Calvi, Corsica, a superb springboard to adventure. Its 1,315 Para-Légionnaires and their comrades of the 3rd and 8th RPIMa (marine paras) can be regarded as the spearhead of the FAR (*Force d'Action Rapide*, France's immediate intervention force).

Should France be drawn into a conflict, it is likely that the REP would be among the first troops to be engaged.

The specialist companies

The REP is structured like all similar French airborne infantry regiments.

Thanks to its light and flexible structure, it can be quickly air-deployed for

Left:
An *Aéronavale* (French Fleet Air Arm) Super Frelon brings in a 120mm mortar team during a training exercise in the scrub-covered Corsican hills.

Below right:
Recce and Support Company badge (top) and Headquarters and Services Company badge (bottom).

Bottom:
With their reputation for professionalism long established, the 'REP men' are often requested to test new weapons on behalf of the French Ordnance or armament manufacturers. A 4th Coy Légionnaire test fires a Belgian-built Minimi light machine gun.

Opposite:
During Exercise Phinia 87, a sniper stalks a party of 'enemy' US Marines from a vantage point. He is armed with the FR-F1 sniping rifle, a weapon since superseded by a more powerful version, the FR-F2.

missions ranging from maintaining order to conventional infantry or light anti-tank combat. Its personnel are experts with all infantry weapons and can operate them in all climates.

Airborne training and routine jumps are made on the regiment's facilities and help maintain a very high '*esprit de corps*'.

The REP has specialised combat companies capable of operating in extreme weather conditions.

Longer service enables the Légionnaires to receive more specialised training than the other categories of paras (conscripts and volunteers).

The first company (identified by a green shoulder strap slip-on loop) specializes in urban and night combat. The second company (red slip-on) is entrusted with mountain warfare. The third (black slip-on) is tasked with amphibious missions, and the fourth (grey slip-on) specialises in sabotage and sniping. These colours are repeated on the triangle sported on the back of the helmet.

During a campaign or on manoeuvres, it is the specialist company's duty to lead the regiment over a specific terrain. For instance, if the REP has the mission to *(continued on page 15)*

FR F-2 SNIPING RIFLE

Superseding the FR F-1, the FR F-2 is a bolt-action rifle issued to sharpshooters.

Calibre: 7.62mm (.308 NATO).

Weight *with stock in composite material, plastic thermal sleeve and bipod* (unloaded): 5.1kg (wooden stock) or 5.3kg (composite stock).

Total lenght: 1,200mm.

Effective range: 800m.

The sight bracket can receive all telescopic sight in use with NATO even though the Fench army prefers a 6x42 telescopic sights for daytime firing and a Gx3 light intensifying sight for night sniping. The rifle can be used without telescopic sight. ❏

THE C.R.A.P.s

Above left:
An REP C.R.A.P. during a free fall. The man wears the orange Gueneau helmet only used in peacetime to avoid mid-air collisions. During their falls, jumpers reach speeds of up to 270km/h.

Left:
Recently paid off, the submarine *Galatée* was often used by the 2e REP C.R.A.P.s for insertions or exfiltrations.

Above right:
A few minutes before the dive, REP C.R.A.P.s fold and store their Zodiac dinghy into a special compartment before receiving the order to climb into the conning tower. The laser sight HK MP-5 submachine gun is ideally suited to the C.R.A.P. recce missions.

Bottom right:
This historic picture shows REP C.R.A.P.s a few moments before they captured As Salman Fort in Iraq. The mission was accomplished in co-operation with the divisional C.R.A.P.s. A short while later, two men from 1er RPIMa (marine paras) were killed on this spot.

Freefalling at night from 6,000 metres to seize an African airport, marking a landing zone in the mountains, blowing up a radar station after insertion in a secluded cove by submarine or more simply hiding and informing on enemy movements are among the missions entrusted to the C.R.A.P.s [1]. With the exception of logistics units, small intelligence and deep penetration commando sections are present in all 11e DP (*Division Parachutiste*, French Airborne Division) regiments.

The two REP C.R.A.Ps. units belong to the discreet but highly efficient special forces family. Superbly trained, they specialise in signals, sabotage, navigation etc. Highly motivated, they tend to shun publicity. Their C.R.A.P. were the only 2e REP elements who took part in the Gulf War.

1. *Commandos de Recherche et d'Action en Profondeur*. It would be highly dangerous for an English-speaker to explain to these super-paras the humour of their acronym.

secure a mountain pass, 2nd Company will open the way.

'A para colonel fights with his Recce and Support Coy'. Often heard in the airborne division, this assertion rings even more true at the REP with its CEA (*compagnie d'éclairage et d'appui*, reconnaissance and support company).

All the equipment of the CEA can be airdropped and its establishment includes a jeep-mounted recce and intelligence platoon, an anti-aircraft platoon with six 20mm guns, a support platoon armed with heavy 120mm mortars towed by Lohr carriers, and two Milan platoons of two pieces each.

The REP also has a Services and Headquarters Company tasked with all clerical duties.

An accomplished sportsman, the airborne Légionnaire can spend his leisure time at a boating club, a parachute club or in various sports halls where martial arts receive special emphasis.

Other peculiarities of the regiment include a parachute maintenance platoon, a dog handling platoon and a military firefighting unit for coping with the forest fires that frequently flare through Corsica.

Opposite, left:
In central Africa a 2e REP 1st Coy VLRA light recce vehicle armed with a .50 machine gun provides fire support for the company combat groups. Africa has always provided the Légion with a privileged training ground.

Above:
Pictured in 1991 on N'Djamena airport, Tchad, this Libyan IL-76 has been sent to repatriate prisoners from Khadaffi's army. They are being closely watched by REP paras.

AFRICAN INTERVENTIONS

Thanks to a clever decolonization policy, France has remained on friendly terms with most of its former African possessions.

As a result, many countries have signed defence agreements with the former colonial power and, in the 1960s, France had to intervene on several occasions when some of her former possessions were threatened by Marxist expansion. In the 1980s, Libya's regional ambitions became the major threat.

Nowadays, the foe is more discreet but no less present on a continent in the throes of political transformation.

Over the past two decades, liberating hostages, evacuating foreign nationals or establishing a defensive screen in the desert have been some of the typical missions entrusted to the Légion.

2e REP, 2e REI, 1er REC, 6e REG and 13e DBLE have lent their efficient support to the following operations:

Djibouti (in 1976 during a hostage seizure at Loyada), *Operation Tacaud* (Tchad, 1978), *Operation Leopard* (Kolwezi,1978), *Operation Baracuda* (Central Africa), *Operation Manta* (Tchad, 1983), *Operation Epervier* (Tchad, 1987), *Operation Requin* (Gabon, 1990), Rwanda (1990), *Operation Baumier* (Zaïre, 1991), *Operation Verdier* (Togo, 1991), *Operation Godoria* (Djibouti, 1991).

In addition to these missions, the Légion was engaged in Lebanon in 1982 during *Operation Epaulard* prior to being attached to the multinational force.

2e REP C.R.A.P members were entrusted with the close protection of Palestinian leader Yasser Arafat when he was evacuated from Beyruth.

In some regiments, even a stranger feels welcome and such is the case with the 2e REI. There, the 'Old Legion' hospitality is a living tradition.

There is no swaggering conceit about the 2e REI; just solid military skill, and confident dignity. 2e REI is a quiet but powerful unit.

Backed up by the largest support company in the French army, 2e REI comprises 1,200 men with 92 armoured vehicles.

The darling of the press during the Gulf intervention, 2e REI made clever use of its public relations office to promote its image and win public sympathy on the eve of its 150th anniversary.

In this regiment the old spirit of the Légion is more alive than in any other unit. Whether in Abéché in the officers' mess or under a tarpaulin flapping in the Arabian wind, nothing has really changed.

True, the armament and the uniforms

2e REI
SHOCK INFANTRY

are of the latest design, but the men as a whole have remained the same. The 'old sweat' cleaning his rifle in the Sahara or in Indochina must have had the same gestures and the same attitude as the tattooed boy oiling his Famas in front of a VAB armoured personnel carrier.

The Warsaw Pact has collapsed and, as a polyvalent unit, 2e REI must adjust to a future where the potential enemy is no longer so clearly designated. In the last years of the 20th century the regiment's assignments may be as varied as conventional warfare in Central Europe, keeping order in Africa or countering a mechanised adversary in the desert.

But 2e REI is fully capable of all these missions, according to a colonel I met. From Tchad to the Gulf, this true warlord always carried Saint Exupery's novel 'Citadelle' in his command vehicle.

In the case of a conflict in Central Europe, 6e DLB (*Division Légère Blindée*, Light Armoured Division) operating within France's Rapid Action Force would launch an anti-tank counter attack and hold off the enemy until the arrival of the main armoured corps.

6e DLB is both a powerful and highly mobile force. Its two infantry regiments, 21e RIMa (marine infantry) and 2e REI (Légionnaires), are equipped with VAB,

VAB

An Infantry Fighting Vehicle, the VAB (*Véhicule de l'Avant Blindé*, or front line armoured vehicle) has four driving wheels (six wheels in export versions) and its welded armour protects the 12 infantrymen it carries from small-arms fire.

Sturdy but comfortable, it is NBC protected and can be transported by plane.

Its cargo or personnel carrier versions can be fitted with turreted or ring mounted 7.62mm or 12.7mm (.50) machine-guns. Ports are provided for individual weapon firing.

Length: 5.980m.
Width: 2.490m.
Height: 2.060m.
Maximum speed: 100km/h.
Speed on water: 7.2km/h.
Water propulsion: hydrojets.
Range: 1,000km.
Fuel capacity (tank under armour): 300l.
Engine: diesel
Power: 162 kW.
Front winch capacity: 7 ton.
Maximum gradient: 60%.
Slope: 35%.

Night driving and firing by means of light intensification episcope and firing telescopes. Smoke dischargers can be used for screening withdrawal . ❏

a vehicle well suited to this type of action.

The VAB is a sturdy, lightly armoured and rugged APC.

Even though it was not designed for desert operations, the VAB gave a good account of itself during Desert Storm. The VAB is on strength with the four rifle companies, the CCS (Headquarters and Services Coy) and the CEA (Recce and Support Coy) of 2e REI.

The 2e REI CEA is the most powerful unit of this type in the French army. Its mortar platoon has been doubled and it has three Milan platoons instead of two.

Top:
Debussing! During Exercise CEITO 89, 1st Coy Légionnaires in NBC suits alight from an APC.
Above:
Corsica, Exercise Phylber 89. In spite of its superlative amphibious capacities, the VAB APC needs to be steered by a good driver during landing operations.

Right:
With the aim of testing 6e DLB amphibious potential, Farfadet exercises are held every two years in the Mediterranean. In 1988, 2e REI is brought ashore by a French Navy EDIC landing craft near Hyères.

'Never was a king, an emperor, a pope or a sultan,
'Guarded by a regiment decked out in gold, scarlet or azure blue,
'With such a proud and manly bearing'.
Excerpt from a poem written by Major Borelli, hero of the 1885 Tuyan Quang siege, and dedicated to his fallen men.

At Abéché, Tchad in 1990, the colonel arrives, the guard presents the arms, and the bugle plays 'Au Caïd'.

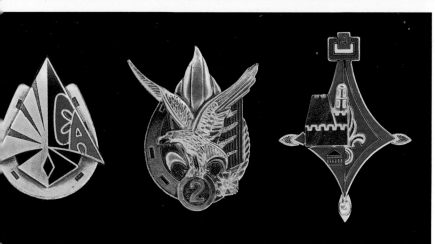

Left to right:
2e REI company badges:
— Headquarters and Services Company
— 2nd Company
— Recce and Support Company
— 3rd Company
— 4th Company.

MILAN

The most powerful anti-tank weapon at the disposal of the French infantry, the Milan is readily portable and can be fired from the ground or from a vehicle. Wire-controlled and fitted with an infra-red guidance system, the Milan can be used as a short-range rocket launcher for anti-tank and 'bunker-busting' tasks. Night-firing capability is granted through addition of the MIRA thermal imaging device allowing for detection at ranges of up to 3,000m and accurate shooting from 1,500m to 2,000m.

Weight (missile and launcher): 11.3kg.
Launcher unit weight: 17kg.
Velocity: 210m/s at 2,000m.
Practical range: 25 to 2,000m.
Penetration: All known armour plating. Propelled by a solid-fuel motor unit. ❑

Top:
Night firing practice for a Milan crew. Night combat experience should prove a definite asset in a war pitting a European army against an African opponent.

Left:
Légionnaires speedily alight from a 2e REI CEA (Recce and Support Coy) VLRA near Abéché.

Below:
In a central Tchad village, headquarters personnel from 2e REI are enquiring about the existence of a track. In Central Africa, the arrival of a French army vehicle is always an event for native populations. '*At least, these soldiers do not beat us*', think the villagers.

Right:
CCS (HQ and Services Coy) jeep driver during a mission near Lake Tchad.

TCHAD

Deep in his heart, each Légionnaire carries a small part of Africa. This is especially true of 2e REI, often on duty in Tchad.

Tchad is a fascinating country, with its sparse trees and sun-scorched immensities where Légionnaires make long rides along dirt tracks at the wheel of battered old jeeps. Its friendly population follow a timeless existence, and always give the men a hearty welcome when they return after a long patrol.

But there is also tension, and the men are often on stand-to. Toyota light trucks have been reported further north and the men are confined to their lines; heavily armed gangs sometimes disturb the peace. Tomorrow may bring a mission. Tonight, there will be no *Gala* at the *Rose des Vents* (names of a popular brand of beer and thelargest pub in N'Djamena). ❑

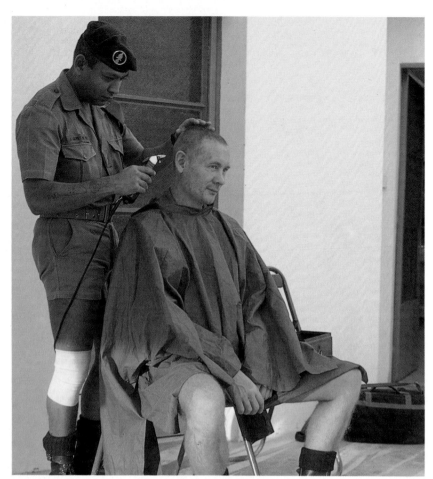

Left:
Haircut 'Légion style' in Tchad. Everyday life in Abéché is hardly different from that in the Quartier Vallorgues in Nîmes. The barber-cum-medic at work.

Below:
Songs always played an important part in the life of the Légion. During an alcohol-free drinking bout in the Saudian sands, Colonel Lecerf strikes up '*Mon régiment*', the 2e REI anthem.

Right above:
Under a portrait of the legendary 'Father of The Legion' Général Rollet, a captain takes care of the administrative tasks of the company. Red-tape is part of of everyday life.

Right below:
During the 150th anniversary celebrations, the 2e REI standard is trooped in front of Tapanar, the mascot mule. This animal is a reminder of the crude but efficient means of Saharan transport often used in the last century by the regiment's glorious forebears.

EVERYDAY LIFE

Out of operations, most of the time is devoted to training or maintaining the equipment.

Even though spare time is available, it is scarce and some Légionnaires may be subject to fits of depression, the famous 'Légion blues' — '*le cafard du Légionnaire*'.

However, the Legion does everything in its power to avoid low morale and reminds its men that respecting the traditions and the '*esprit de corps*' should contribute to making every Légionnaire feel at home. Celebrations are frequent and the opportunities for having a drink numerous.

During these drinking bouts, the Légionnaires sing their superb traditional songs...or some more rowdy numbers in their repertoire. ❐

1er REC

'In Syria, the Foreign Legion
Advances through the desert.
Sperheading the column
Is the 1er Etranger de Cavalerie.'

(Excerpt from the 1er REC war-song)

Nowadays, whenever a mechanised enemy has to be countered, 1er REC is still 'spearheading the column'. In Iraq or Tchad they follow in the hoofprints of their forebears who pacified Syria and Morocco in the 1920s and 1930s.

Created in 1921, 1er REC is one of the most ancient and endearing units of the Foreign Legion. The staff of the *Royal Etranger de Cavalerie* are both légion-naires and cavalrymen.

Blending the traditions of both services in a modern context of efficiency sums up the REC spirit.

The tank turrets may be bristling with laser range-finders and the guns firing APDS, but horsehair plumes are still atta-ched to the squadron standards standing in front of the captain's tent.

Hands are grimy but silver [1] is eve-rywhere, on the uniforms and in the mess. There is no pedantry and each visitor is welcomed like an honoured guest.

But the REC also means firepower and mobility, with 36x105mm guns and 12x HOT-fitted VABs capable of covering

---

1. By tradition, the metal of buttons and rank stripes in the French cavalry, instead of gold in most other branches.

AMX-10 RC

The AMX-10 RC is a 6x6 wheeled armoured reconnaissance vehicle with anti-tank capacity. Its tactical cross-country mobility can be compared with with that of tracked vehicles and it is amphibious without preparation.

Weight (combat order)**:** 16 tons.
Length: 5.94m.
Height: 2.06m.
Maximum road speed: 85km/h.
Average cross-country speed: 40km/h.
Speed in water: 7.5km/h.
Water propulsion: hydrojets.
Range: 1,000km.

Combat autonomy: 26 hours.
Gradient: 50%.
Slope: 30%.
Armament: one 105mm calibre gun, one 7.62mm coaxially-mounted machine gun, 4 smoke dischargers.
Crew: four (one tank commander, one gunner, one loader, one driver).

Suited for day and night combat through a fire control system with magnifying rangefinder telescope. NBC protected, the AMX-10 RC can cross rivers and waterways of moderate difficulty under its own power and without preparation. ❏

THE LEGION'S MAILED FIST

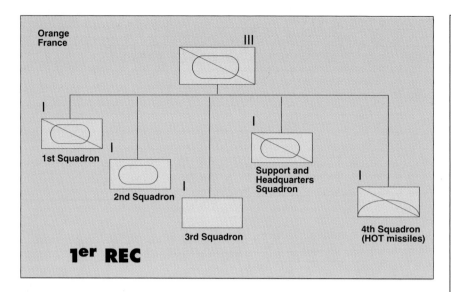

Orange
France

III

1st Squadron

2nd Squadron

3rd Squadron

Support and
Headquarters
Squadron

4th Squadron
(HOT missiles)

1ᵉʳ REC

VAB-HOT

The VAB-HOT is a wheeled, armoured anti-tank vehicle designed to destroy tanks at long range. It is fitted with the Mephisto Euromissile retractable launcher, firing HOT missiles at ranges of up to 4,000m. The retractable launcher system grants the vehicle superiority in the following fields:

Concealment: when the launcher is retracted, the VAB-HOT is practically indistinguishable from the APC version.

Crew protection: missiles can be reloaded inside the vehicle without exposing its crew to enemy fire or contamination.

Length: 5.980m.

Width: 2.490m.

Height (launcher retracted): 2.060m.

Speed: 100km/h (in water: 7.2km/h).

Water propulsion: hydrojets.

Range: 1,000km.

Armoured fuel tank contents: 300l.

Armament: 4 HOT anti-tank missiles with automatic wire-controlled infrared guidance. A 7.5mm machine gun mounted on the front right-hand side for close defence.

Missile reserve: minimum 12.

Crew: four. The missile system can be operated by one man.

The VAB-HOT is NBC protected.

An observation turret rotating through a 270° arc is fitted on the rear deck of the vehicle. ❐

800km in one day.

In central Europe during Operation Kecker Spatz, in Tchad during the Ati charge, or more recently during the offensive in Iraq, the REC has shown that it is the iron fist of the Légion.

Some 41 officers, 141 NCOs and 647 Légionnaires are serving with honour and loyalty in the REC's three armoured squadrons, one anti-tank squadron and one headquarters squadron.

The standard mount of the REC is the AMX-10 RC, a powerful and agile vehicle fitted with a 105mm gun. Amphibious, this 'wheeled tank' is capable of fighting in NBC environment. Each squadron currently fields 12 AMX-10 RC. During the Gulf war, additional armour had to be fitted by REC or divisional field workshops.

The anti-tank squadron numbers 12 Mephisto-turretted VAB-HOT fitted with four missiles. After a 17-second flight,

Below:
During Exercise Farfadet, a 10 RC alighting from a COTAM (French Air Transport Command) C-160 Transall near Perpignan, Southern France. Highly airmobile, an REC squadron can be deployed overseas in a matter of hours.

Right:
Perfectly camouflaged and fitted with a 12.7mm heavy machine gun, a P-4 light field car waiting for orders during Exercise Dragon Hammer. A platoon comprises two P-4 and three AMX-10 RC.

Below right:
A VAB-HOT displays its clout as the commander looks for prey in the Saudi desert. In the offensive phase of Operation Daguet, 1er REC VAB-HOTs distinguished themselves during the capture of As Salman airfield, in Iraq.

PEUGEOT P-4 FIELD VEHICLE

VLTT (*véhicule léger tous terrains*) Peugeot P-4 is a 4x4 cross-country tactical vehicle issued to all French army units. Multipurpose, fast and reliable, it can fulfil all the tasks entrusted to a light military vehicle such as recce, liaison, etc.

Available in three versions armed with Milan, 12.7mm or 7.62mm machine guns.

Weight (combat order): 1,895kg.

Weight (laden): 2,495kg.
Width: 1.70m.
Length: 4.20m.
Height (laden): 1.90m.
Speed: 108km/h.
Range (with jerrycan contents): 660km.
Gradient: 50%.
Slope: 30%.
Fording depth: 0.50m.
Engine: Peugeot 4 in-line cylinder 2.498 cm3 XD-3 diesel engine.
Seating capacity: six. ❏

Top:
Codenamed 'Miramar', the French deployment zone in Saudi Arabia was remarkably well suited for manoeuvring. In the photograph, 1st Squadron 10-RCs thundering through the desert. The ball compass mounted on the turret next to the sighting telescope proved very efficient.

Right:
Small Peugeot motorbikes are used for liaison or reconnaissance. During Dragon Hammer in Sicily, a motorcyclist transmits a message to the regimental HQ.

Overleaf, left:
REC Squadron badges.
From top to bottom: ECS (HQ and Services Sqn), 1st Squadron, 2nd Squadron, 3rd Squadron, and 4th Squadron.

Overleaf, main photo:
With its trim vane erected, an AMX-10 RC from 1st Squadron crosses a lake during the winter of 1990. The 10 RC is amphibious without preparation. A few months later, in a sand camouflage colour, the same vehicle helped overrun As Salman.

the HOT missile can pulverise any existing tank over a 4,000m range.

The 4th Squadron HOT-fitted VAB received its baptism of fire during the capture of As Salman airfield, in which several dug-in tanks were destroyed.

The 1er REC is also equipped with P-4 light field vehicles fitted with .50 machine guns, and motorcyclists acting as the 'eyes and ears' of the squadron.

ACTION IN THE GULF

On 2 August 1990, many Légionnaires watching the news on television saw Saddam Hussein's troops invade Kuwait. This was the main topic in the mess rooms, though few of them could have guessed that six months later, they would find themselves in Iraq.

On 30 September 1990 at Yambu, the ferry 'Corse' unloaded the advanced elements of 2e REI and a 1er REC squadron assigned to the 1er Spahis.

Three days later, after a 3,000 km trek across the desert, the French forces established themselves at Arenas, 60km from the Iraqi border.

Saddam's divisions could have pounced on them any time and without warning. Reinforcements soon arrived and a GMLE (*Groupement de Marche de la Légion Etrangère,* Légion Task Force) was formed. Meanwhile, the French withdrew further south in Miramar where intensive training was pursued.

Early in January, 15 days before the ultimatum expired, GMLE comprised the following units: 2e REI (with the exception of the 1st Company on duty in Gabon), 1er REC, 6e REG (engineers), one 1er RE combat company and the 2e REP C.R.A.Ps.

On 17 January 1991, in spite of continuous Scud alarms, GMLE and other French troops left Miramar and made for Rhafa, their assembly zone facing Iraq.

In February, a firefight took place with an Iraqi patrol. Supported by fire provided by 11e RAMa (marine artillery), 2e REI engaged the enemy. Two days before the major allied offensive, 2e REI supported by a 6e REG company captured their objective, an Iraqi border post codenamed *Nachez*.

On the 23rd, the headlong rush started with the French forces forming a two-pronged column.

On the 'Beaulieu' axis, the column of which GMLE formed part, was tasked with capturing As Salman airport. This airfield was to be used later as a support base for the US XVIII Airborne Corps heading for the Euphrates.

What followed is now history. Supported by American A-10s and the 11e RAMa's 155mm TRF-1 howitzers, GMLE knocked out a poorly motivated enemy taken aback by the mobility of the formation.

In less than 50 hours, the objective codenamed *White* (the airport) had been secured and GMLE, westernmost unit of the allied forces, had thrust 150km into Iraq.

The Légionnaires had captured hundreds of prisoners and seized large quantities of material including armoured vehicles. But more important, no casualties were suffered and no material damage was sustained.

The bulk of GMLE returned to France in March, and a rapturous welcome awaited the Légionnaires.

Only a few 6e REG parties were left in Iraq and Kuwait for mine clearing. During one of these missions, *Adjudant-Chef* Sudre from 6e REG met with a soldier's death.

Top:
Miramar. Less than 80km from the Iraqi border, 2e REI infantrymen training in an unfamiliar terrain. The desert camouflage outfits have not yet been issued.

Right:
25 February 1991. During their advance along the 'Texas Axis', Capitaine Kjan's 'scuba-sappers' from 6e REG DINOPS captured dozens of Iraqis.

6e REG

Created on 1st July 1984, the 6e Régiment Etranger de Génie is the newest of all Légion regiments, but heir to the traditions of the 6e REI (*Régiment du Levant*) that won fame during the Syrian campaign in 1941.

Attached to 6e DLB (Light Armoured Division), 6e REG is a dynamic and modern force, though a worthy heir to the traditions inherited from the companies of 'builder Légionnaires' who created modern Algeria.

Clearing obstacles, assisting during difficult crossings or erecting obstacles during withdrawal are some of the missions entrusted to the 6e REG. To accomplish its tasks, the Légion's assault engineer regiment is organised into three sapper companies, one support company and one headquarters and services company.

The Légionnaires of 6e REG are highly skilled specialists trained for the limited but brutal actions carried out by the sapper companies, transported in VABs as they spearhead the advanced elements of 6e DLB.

The assault sappers have the job of clearing the way under enemy fire and are

thoroughly familiar with flame throwers and breaching or cutting charges. The REG certainly fields the largest number of specialists within the Légion including bridge layers, drivers, mine clearing experts, combat divers, flame thrower operators and construction engineers.

Like all metropolitan Légion units, 6e REG sends rotating companies overseas. Without neglecting their military training, they put their building skills to good use in the Republic of Central Africa, Mayotte and Guyana. Like the Roman legions of old, the regiment thus exercises its functions full-time even when the other units are not on operations.

These missions include mine clearing or cleaning up operations in countries devastated by war. With the 17e Génie ('regular' army), 6e REG cleared mines in Beirut, Faya Largeau, Djibouti and Kuwait City. Several Légionnaires and NCOs were killed during these dangerous and obscure missions.

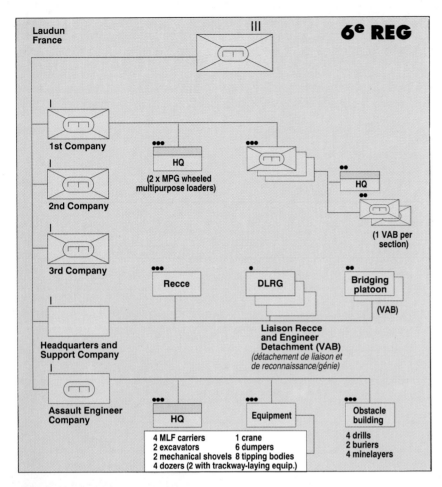

**Laudun
France**

III

6ᵉ REG

1st Company

2nd Company

3rd Company

**Headquarters and
Support Company**

**Assault Engineer
Company**

HQ
(2 x MPG wheeled
multipurpose loaders)

HQ

(1 VAB per
section)

Recce

DLRG

**Bridging
platoon**
(VAB)

**Liaison Recce
and Engineer
Detachment (VAB)**
*(détachement de liaison et
de reconnaissance/génie)*

HQ

Equipment

**Obstacle
building**

4 MLF carriers   1 crane
2 excavators   6 dumpers
2 mechanical shovels 8 tipping bodies
4 dozers (2 with trackway-laying equip.)

4 drills
2 buriers
4 minelayers

Below:
**Another of the regiment's special skills is
fighting in built-up areas and clearing enemy
booby traps and ordnance.**

Right:
**'Fire in the hole !'. The sappers of the
6e REG are masters of all the elements :
earth, air, fire and water. A twist of the wrist
combines the first three.**

In 1989, the 6e REG took part in Operation Salaam in Pakistan and Légionnaires trained Afghan mujahideen to defu-
se Soviet ordnance. During the Gulf war,
6e REG was the spearhead on the 'Beaulieu' and 'Texas' penetration routes and
paved the way for one of the US 82nd
Airborne units. Many prisoners were captured during this action.

The structure of 6e REG is unique in
the French forces. It is equipped to fight
like a conventional unit while blazing a
trail for the division across the most varied
terrains and obstacles.

It is capable of clearing a path on a landing beach, widening a mountain road,
exploring a river bank, digging trenches
for an infantry regiment, destroying or
building a bridge or erecting impassible
obstacles crammed with diabolical booby
traps.

The rifle companies use engineer VAB
vehicles and comprise two platoons, respectively equipped with the equipment

Left, above: **The 'sapeur légionnaire' is a young man with nerves of steeel. Here, 3rd Coy assault pioneers carrying bangalore charges used to blast a path though barbed wire entanglements.**

Left, below:
Carrying a canvas trackway, a bulldozer paves the way for landing troops during Exercise Farfadet 90.

Top: **The responsibilities and the concentration required of sappers are etched on the faces of these 3rd Coy members.**

Bottom: **Mine-clearance training with Kevlar helmet and special armour.**

REG company badges.
From top to bottom:
– 1st Company.
– 3rd Company *(left)* **– 2nd Company** *(right)***.**
– Headquarters and Services Company.
– Support Company.

41

After their defeat, withdrawing Iraqis left behind thousands of mines and booby traps in Kuwait City. With their 17e RG counterparts, 6e REG sappers cleared the beaches and the sea front. Training paid off — but Légionnaires died nonetheless.
(Courtesy Eric Micheletti)

DINOPS COMBAT DIVERS

Operating within its Recce and Support Company, 6e REG fields some of the Légion's most highly trained personnel: the SAF/TSIO [1] diver/paratroopers.

Originally, 6e REG only had a few divers tasked with assisting its vehicles across rivers. Their mission consisted of exploring the river banks to assess whether they were suitable for armoured crossing, and rescuing the crews in case of difficulties.

Under the guidance of dynamic officers, these units were beefed up and the scope of their missions widened to include beach recce, mine clearing and sabotage.

Airdropped or inserted by submarines, helicopters or kayaks, the diver/paratroopers are capable of swimming for three hours twenty feet below the surface and covering six kilometers to plant a charge or prepare a landing.

Equipped with 'oxygers' (closed circuit breathing apparatus) and special weapons such as the sound-suppressed MP-5 Heckler and Koch, they often work in the Mediterannean with the American SEALs and RECON as well as their prestigious Italian or Spanish counterparts.

During Operation Daguet, the divers performed conventional sapper duties on the 'Texas' penetration route and opened the way for the US 82nd Airborne Division.

Some time later, they became reacquainted with the water when they decontaminated Kuwait City Harbour in the company of Australian divers.

---

1. *Sections d'aide au franchissement/Travaux subaquatiques et interventions offensives*, i.e. river crossing assistance/underwater offensive missions.

6e REG para-diver badge

Right:
Night infiltration with kayaks, a discreet and efficient method used by British commandos during World War Two.

Above: **Night vision goggles, Goretex outfit and top physical shape contribute to the preparedness of DINOPs.**
Below:
Providing assistance to tanks during river crossings remains one of the main tasks entrusted to divers; the crew of this AMX-10 RC are in safe hands.

DESERT SENTRIES

As he leaves the plane at Djibouti airport, the Légionnaire transferred to the '13th' immediately knows what's in store for him. He is assaulted by a sultry atmosphere, mingling the breath of the monsoon with undertones of the arid desert.

With its temperature around 40°, Djibouti is at the crossroads between Africa, the Middle East and the Indies. This unique location grants the Republic of Djibouti a paramount strategic importance as it controls the outlet to the Red Sea.

As a result of defence agreements, France maintains a large body of troops on the young republic's territory, and 13e DBLE is one of the pillars of the garrison.

Djibouti offers the Légionnaires totally different surroundings. The town itself looks like all the former French Empire garrison towns where the Legion and the 'Colo' were entrusted with the defence of the frontiers; and to the present day, Djibouti has retained much of its old colonial character.

After leaving the Quartier Monclar, the Légionnaire must haggle with the cab driver over the fare. Then, he may enjoy a local fish dish, the '*poisson aux caisses*' in a restaurant, unless he settles for a grouper, skewered tortoise at Massuf's or an Ethiopian tropical fish.

During the meal on the terrace, the man is constantly harrassed by hawkers. The end of the evening is spent in any one of a dozen picturesque and colourful bars *(Continued on page 50)*

(Continued on page 50)

Above:
The white képi was not meant to be worn in a tank turret, but on receipt of their new Sagaie fighting vehicles in 1987, the men lost no time posing on their new steeds with their traditional headgear.

Right:
Swift and deft landing for 13e DBLE 3rd Coy Légionnaires.

Overleaf:
VLRA-mounted .50 heavy machine-guns provide covering fire for these Légionnaires storming a position during a training exercise on the Myriam site. The man in the foreground is armed with an 89mm LRAC.

13e DBLE

where 'naias', superb Somali or Ethiopian girls, help the Légionnaires forget their troubles.

But 13e DBLE activities are of course not restricted to tourism and pub crawls. It is primarily a redoubtable fighting unit operating in one of the planet's harshest climates. After leaving the town and its cosmopolitan populace, the Légionnaire finds himself in a stony, prehistoric universe where overstretching one's limits seems the normal thing to do.

This arid land can only support stunted, sparse scrub and the Légion becomes reacquainted with its Saharan past during long border patrols in the heat and dust. At night

Operating VLRAs, these 13e DBLE columns are reminiscent of the Légion saga in the Western Desert, 1941-43, when this regiment fought alongside the British 8th Army.

Below: **the unit has been granted extended reach through the addition of Milan, capable of destroying a tank at 2,000m.**

Right and below:
**One of the 13e DBLE support company
120mm mortars is readied for action and
fired.**

120 mm MORTAR

The Hotchkiss-Brandt 120mm mortar is one of the best weapons of its class in the world. Its bombs have practically the same destructive power as 155mm ordnance.

The crew are trained to set up their piece, fire and withdraw in less than 10 minutes.

The mortar can be towed, carried inside a helicopter or slung under it.

Each Légion infantry unit has six 120mm mortars, and 2e REI twice this number. The range is 12 kilometres. ❒

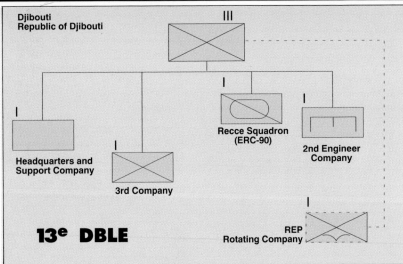

13e DBLE

Djibouti
Republic of Djibouti

Headquarters and
Support Company

3rd Company

Recce Squadron
(ERC-90)

2nd Engineer
Company

REP
Rotating Company

thorn scrub crackles in the campfires and lone sentries gaze at an immense starry sky. Here, man returns to his origins.

In Djibouti, the silence of the desert prevails; but sometimes the crack of an automatic weapon and the shouts of defeated enemies echo down the wind.

In 1976, at Loyada, the armoured vehicles of the recce squadron came to grips with Somali border guards when children were taken hostage. Over the last few years, the '13th' has often stood-to at the borders; and in autumn 1990, it had the privilege of disarming its potential foe, the Ethiopian army, whose debris, still dangerous, fled towards Djibouti. These operations were codenamed *Totem* and *Godoria*. As the year 2000 draws nearer, the 13e DBLE Légionnaires remain prepared to prove worthy heirs of their famed predecessors of Narvik, Bir Hakeim or Dien Bien Phu.

To fulfil its missions in the 'horn of Africa', 13e DBLE fields specialised companies. It is the only all-arms regiment in the Legion, fielding sappers, infantrymen and cavalrymen. Based at the Quartier Monclar, the 13e DBLE consists of :

— HQ, Services and Support Company, including a Milan platoon and a 120mm Brandt mortar platoon.

— 2nd Engineer Company contributes its earth moving equipment for the benefit of the French garrison or units of the host country.

— 3rd Rifle Company comprises three VLRA-mounted rifle platoons. These platoons are capable not only of infantry combat but also have specialised skills : respectively, recce divers, demolition experts and snipers.

Left:
13e DBLE Recce Squadron ERC-90 Sagaies during a landing exercise in the Tajiourah gulf.
(Courtesy 'Képi Blanc')

ERC-90 SAGAIE

The Sagaie was designed for reconnaissance missions over large areas and the destruction of enemy infiltrations. Ideally suited for desert operations, the Sagaie only requires light support resources and has the enormous advantage of being air-transportable.

Weight (in combat order): 8,300kg.
Speeds: 95km/h (on road), 7.2km/h in water.
Length: 7.68m.
Width: 2.50m.
Height: 2.32m.
Gradient: 50%.
Slope: 30%.
Fording depth: 1m.
Vertical obstacle: 0.80m.
Range: 700km (at 60km/h).
Armament: 90mm F 4 gun with a 3,000m maximum range, one co-axially-mounted 7.62mm machine gun and one close defence 7.62mm machine gun.
Crew: one commander, one gunner, one driver.
Power unit: one 2,800 cm3 V6 PRV petrol engine developing 106 kW.
Water propulsion: hydrojets.   ❑

Top:
In Djibouti, a 2e REP para on guard duty. The Légionnaire belongs to a rotation company, one of which is normally attached to the 13th.

Left:
In anticipation of Camerone Day celebrations, this Légionnaire is growing a beard.

Opposite, below:
13e DBLE badges:
— **Headquarters and Support Company**
— **2nd Engineer Company**
— **Recce Squadron**
— **3rd Company.**

— the Reconnaissance Squadron is based at Oueah, 37km from Djibouti, and operates 12 x ERC-Sagaie and a VLRA-mounted platoon.

The '13th' also has a rotating company from 2e REP, generally based at Arta.

As always, training is permanent, and maximum effort is expected from the Légionnaires during their hours of duty. Because of the harshness of the climate, the siesta is uniquely authorised to the French troops based in Djibouti.

The Légion also runs the Arta Plage (Arta Beach) training centre used by both Djiboutian and French forces.

3e REI

France's future, and possibly that of the Old Continent, may be decided in Guyana, home to the Kuru Space Centre and Europe's most precious asset in the space race.

Located on the Equator, this superb launching base is guarded by one of the Légion's most prestigious regiments: 3e REI. Created as the RMLE, or '*Régiment de Marche de la Légion Etrangère*' in 1915 from the remnants of several 'régiments de marche' badly mauled early in the First World War, the regiment was commanded in 1917 by Colonel Rollet, regarded as the founder of the modern-day Légion.

A regiment of high traditions and the second most decorated unit of the French army [1], the 3e Régiment Etranger is closely linked with the European space adventure.

Its men are tasked with guarding the installations as well as maintaining a presence in this sole French possession on the South American continent.

'*The jungle is demanding and worthy of a Légionnaire*' a CEFE [2] instructor told me.

At the end of the 20th century, 'the 3rd' have a unique challenge, flying 'ultra-lite' aircraft, manning 20mm guns, or riding dugouts on the Oyapock River.

Fanned by highly motivated officers, the Legion spirit burns as brightly by a

---

1. After the RICM, the former *Régiment d'infanterie coloniale du Maroc*, now *Régiment d'infanterie et chars de marine*, a Marine infantry regiment once raised in Morocco.

2. *Centre d'Entraînement en Forêt Equatoriale*, Equatorial Forest Training Centre.

Above, left:
Sine 1945, the 3e has spent most of its service in the tropics: in Indochina, then after the Algerian War in Madagascar, and finally in Guyana.

Left:
3e Régiment Etranger d'Infanterie badges: From left to right and from top to bottom: Headquarters and Services Company, 2nd Company, Recce and Support Company, 3rd Company.

Right:
Three days before an *Ariane* launch, everything is under control and the countdown has already started. No unauthorized person will be allowed near the launching pad.

THE GATES OF OUTER SPACE

LEGIO
PATRIA NOSTRA

3ᵉ R.E.I

As often seen in the Légion, 3e REI offers a blend of modern and traditional equipment.

Right:
A 20mm anti-aircraft gun and its crew stand ready to defend the site against attacks by low-flying aircraft.

Below, right:
In the vicinity of the European space installation, a 3e REI platoon is heliborne during a training exercise.

Opposite:
Crammed to overflowing with Légionnaires, a dugout sails down the Maroni River during one of the famous 'in-depth' missions carried out by the 3e REI through the Guyanese jungle.

campfire in the rain forest as in the pyramid-shaped mess of the Quartier Forget.

Lack of away-from-home allowance and a high cost of living (Guyana is a French department) do not deter many NCOs from seeking a posting with the 3e REI. The reason is that this regiment has maintained a unique spirit.

Topography strongly influences the two types of missions entrusted to 3e REI. To protect Kuru and its vital installations, 3e REI fields light motorised companies equipped with flexible armament well-suited to the terrain.

During *Ariane* launches, 81mm mortars, 20mm guns and two 'ultra-lites' (excellent for spotting flights) are deployed around the base. For its movements, the unit makes use of rivers and waterways, the only communication links with the back country.

3e REI has a flotilla of large dugouts sporting the Légion colours and rowed by oarsmen who still believe in the spirits of the river.

The regiment comprises :
— Headquarters and Services Coy.
— the 2nd Rifle Company, specially trained for the defence of the Kuru base. This company also maintains the 'ultra-lites' and trains sharpshooters.
— the 3rd Company is tasked with all the missions pertaining to river activities and also trains hand-to-hand fighting instructors.
— the Recce and Support Company (CEA) has a scout and reconnaissance platoon, a 20mm gun platoon for air defence and an engineering platoon. As Guyana is still a virgin country, the struggle against encroaching vegetation is constant and this engineering platoon is constantly called upon to intervene.

During the rocket launches, an extra company may be provided but docs not necessarily come from the Légion.

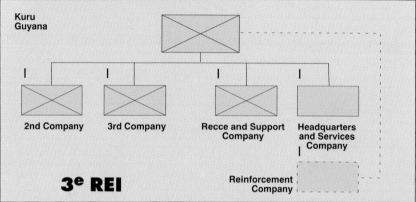

Kuru
Guyana

2nd Company   3rd Company   Recce and Support Company   Headquarters and Services Company

Reinforcement Company

3ᵉ REI

Above: lightning visit to an 'in-depth patrol' by the unit commander. Using chainsaws and explosives, the Légionnaires have cleared the ground for the helicopter that will deliver mail, orders and fresh food.

Left: sweat streams down the face of a Légionnaire during an 'in-depth' mission. In jungle or desert conditions, the men must drink a great deal of water.

Right: the hunting was good and tonight, toucan will be on the menu.

Right, inset: traditional picture in Guyana. A Regina instructor handling a king python. Legionnaires receive tuition on all types of reptiles they'll encounter on their deep missions in the jungle.

During his stint in Guyana, the Légionnaire will certainly have a chance of taking part in a deep mission that will take him to the remotest part of the country.

The aim of these missions can be land surveying, patrolling, flag-showing or fighting smugglers.

The mission can last several weeks and the Légionnaires take the maximum cargo. Dugouts are used for the first leg of the trek, and they must often be carried on the men's backs as they set off on foot through the Amazonian jungle.

In this stifling universe the jaguar and the anaconda are almost harmless in comparison with the permanent humidity and insects. Top physical shape is a prerequisite as the jungle proves unforgiving to those unfamiliar with its rigours.

Supplies are brought in by helicopter but the Légionnaires must prepare the landing zone with explosives and chainsaws. During deep missions the men live off the land and peccaries, hogs, iguanas and caimans often supplement the Légionnaires' larder. At long last, the men reach an Oyampi Indian village and the smile of a child rewards those who have conquered the rain forest.

Right:
At Regina, a Spanish-born instructor has just demonstrated his expertise and leadership abilities on the obstacle course. In a few moments, trainees will take over.

Below:
Neck-deep in the mud, a trainee is put through his paces: a daily sight at Regina.

Opposite:
In the Amazonian rain forest, temperatures reach 40° C and the air is saturated with moisture. In such conditions, carrying a man on one's back along a slippery path is no easy task.

REGINA, RAIN FOREST TRAINING CENTRE

High on a hill overlooking the Approuague River, Szuts Camp is home to one of the top jungle commando training centres, second only to the Manaus school in Brazil.

Set in scenery of breath-taking beauty and run by the 3e REI, this centre is the envy of foreign armies.

Here, professionals with more than 15 years jungle experience teach all the techniques necessary to overcome the traps of the Amazonian rain forest.

Trainees come from the French but also from American, Canadian, Dutch and Brazilian forces. During their three-week training period, the trainees sweat blood.

The curriculum is comprehensive and leaves the trainees no respite; it includes forest movement, firing practice from dugouts or jungle tracks, bridging techniques, jungle and mud track movement, traps, survival, and obstacle course, completed with tuition on the fauna and flora.

All the Légionnaires transferred to the 3e REI have one or two spells at Regina during their posting in Guyana.

5e RE

'A mountain stood in the way.
The order was given to proceed.
So the Légion went through.'

Commemorating the building in 1933 of the Foum-Zabel tunnel in Morocco, this inscription sums up the qualities of 5e RE.

In 1963, after a brilliant campaign in Algeria where the traditions of Tonkin were upheld, the first element of the future 5e RE landed in Polynesia. Originally known as 5e Régiment Mixte du Pacifique, the unit received its final designation in 1984.

Everything had to be built from scratch on the remote coral atoll of Mururoa; and the Légion proceeded with its task 19,000 km away from France. Mururoa lies 1,200 km even from Tahiti.

True to their reputation of 'légionnaires bâtisseurs' (builders), the men of the '5th' built most of the CEP installation (*Centre d'Expérimentation du Pacifique*) where French nuclear weapons were to be tested. When construction was complete, the regiment was maintained there to protect the facilities.

The Légion tackles every task on the island: de-salinating water, unloading freighters, mixing concrete, ensuring the security and safety of supply planes, blasting coral, building roads — and fighting if necessary. Jacks of all trades, the 5e RE Légionnaires are isolated for two years on the atoll. Every eight weeks, the men are granted a six-day furlough in Tahiti.

Although the 5e RE Légionnaire is primarily a builder, he is also a fighter. Numerous landing exercises, Zodiac raids or tactical lifts in Super Puma helicopters help keep the men at a high level of proficiency.

Apart from its Headquarters and Services Company (CCS), the 5e RE comprises the following units:

— an Engineer Company (CG, or *compagnie de génie*) tasked with public works and concrete mixing.

— a Rifle and Heavy Works Company (CCT, or *compagnie de combat et de travaux*) tasked with heavy engineering work

Above:
The flexibility of air transport enables the Légion to intervene on all the coral islands composing French Polynesia. This type of intervention receives special attention from 5e RE 'caravelle' companies and is the subject of intense training.

Left:
5e RE Légionnaires can build just about anything, anywhere.

Right:
Late briefing for these 5e RE Légionnaires before a night operation. Combat skills are never neglected, whatever a Légion unit's primary task. *(Courtesy* Képi Blanc)

and defence missions on Mururoa and throughout Polynesia.

— a Transport and Maintenance Company (CTR, or *compagnie de transport et de réparation*) entrusted with transport, shipping and equipment maintenance and repair.

Another company, the CBS (*compagnie de base et des sites*) providing specialised and clerical staff, answers to 5e RE but its personnel are drawn from the French regular army with the exception of a few 'cadres' who belong to the Légion.

63

Mayotte is a volcanic island standing in one of the world's largest lagoons.

This idyllic site is part of the Comores archipelago that controls the Strait of Mozambique, halfway between the African coast and Madagascar.

This strait has enormous strategic importance, as every day giant tankers carrying crude oil from the Middle East must pass through this channel.

Should the Suez Canal be blocked as a result of a war, all the traffic from the Middle East to Europe would have to pass through the Mozambique Channel.

In 1974, when the Comores became independent, the population expressed its wish to remain linked with France; and in a referendum held in 1976, it decided to remain part of the French Republic.

Since then a small Légion detachment has been kept on the island, even though the arrival of the first Légionnaires on the Dzaoudzi Rocks dates back to 1967 (it was a 3e REI company based in Madagascar).

At the end of 1973, the '3rd' left for Guyana and the detachment posted on the Comores became known as DLEC (*Détachement de la Légion Etrangère aux Comores*), and later DLEM (*Détachmeent de la Légion Etrangère à Mayotte*) when the Comores became independent in 1974.

DLEM comprises a headquarters and services element (ECS) and a rotating company provided either by the Légion or by another regiment from the 11th Parachute Division.

DLEM has the mission of maintaining a French presence in the Indian Ocean, an area of vital strategic importance.

Since 1984, DLEM has been entrusted with the standard of the 2e REC, a Légion cavalry unit disbanded after the Algerian War.

Left:
Badge worn by the Foreign Legion Detachment on Mayotte.

Below:
As a result of improved relationships between France and Madagascar, DLEM 'cadres' and Légionnaires have recently spent a few days with the Madagascan army. On the large Indian Ocean island, a Légionnaire tests a Soviet-made Dragunov sniping rifle.

Right:
During a rotation on Mayotte, REC cavalrymen turned themselves into marines and captured a beach without support from their tanks.
(Courtesy Képi Blanc*)*

DLEM
FOREIGN LEGION
DETACHMENT ON MAYOTTE

'Légionnaire who are you, Légionnaire, where are you bound?
- I go where adventures await me.'

Excerpt from *'Cravate Verte et Képi Blanc'*, a Légion marching song.

ACKNOWLEDGEMENTS

I would need a whole book to thank all those who lent me their support in the preparation of these two albums.

I beg forgiveness from those I might have forgotten. One day, we'll meet again at the 'popote' and I'll settle my debts.

The Légion is a reflection of its chief and I address my heartfelt thanks to Général Le Carre who made this project posible.

My thanks also to Colonel André, former Public Relations Officer, who made me share his love for the Légion before his untimely disappearance. I also wish to extend my gratitude to the following Public Relations Officers: Colonel Tomati and Colonel Leroy. My thanks also to unit commanders Vabinski, Koevoet, Gausseresse, Ivanov, Soubirou and Derville, modern-day 'condottieri'.

The 'grands adjoints', and more specially Colonel Lecerf and Colonel Mariotti, 'grands seigneurs' in all times and places.

Major Guarmer, Major Deutshman and Major Lallemand who, although snowed under with paper work, persuaded me to take part in their morning jog.

Capitaine Toulin, Capitaine Baudart, Capitaine Kjan, Capitaine Boulet, Capitaine Dumont Saint-Priest for their polite welcome to the 'kingdom' of their companies.

I also express my indebtness to the lieutenants, too numerous to be individually named here. Generally harsh to journalists (aren't they, Lieutenant Gillet?), they have upheld against all odds an undying ideal through all the uncertainties of modern life.

Those who keep the Légion going shouldn't be forgotten either, the 'adjudants' and other 'sous-officiers' who, in all simplicity, contributed their efficiency to the pages of this book. Adjudant Susa and Maréchal des Logis Stoeng deserve a special mention.

I also wish to extend my gratitude to the 'caporaux-chefs', 'caporaux' and 'légionnaires' with whom I shared many a bottle of beer in sometimes unusual conditions.

I am also indebted to Colonel Terrasson, the Légion's 'living encyclopaedia', and to the Képi Blanc editorial team who supplied some of the photographs.

Last but not least, the SIRPA Terre where the Képis Blancs are largely represented, and more specially Colonel Pinart-Legris and Capitaine Margail.

Also available
THE FRENCH FOREIGN LEGION TODAY

DESIGN, LAY OUT AND GRAPHICS
Jean-Marie MONGIN and Philippe TEULE / HISTOIRE & COLLECTIONS – PARIS

© 1992 - Yves Debay.

Printed in Italy.

This edition published in Great Britain 1992 by Windrow & Greene Ltd.
5, Gerrard Street
London W1V 7LJ

ISBN 1-872004-97-0